# this is what
## what
## my soul
## looks like

SHARON JONES

A catalogue record for this book is available from the British Library.

First Edition 2020.

First published in Great Britain in 2020 by Carpet Bombing Culture.

An imprint of Pro-actif Communications.

Email books@carpetbombingculture.co.uk

©Sharon Jones

ISBN: 978-1-908211-89-7

Cover illustration: Markovka/Shutterstock

www.carpetbombingculture.co.uk

the future
is
unwritten

# Thinking:

# The talking of the soul with itself

Plato

Me

*Just who am I?*

Life

You

*Who's here with me?*

# Self reflection: empathy for the soul

# *an imminent connection*

In handwriting there is *presence*. For this reason the soul searching you document within this book is captured as a piece of evidence, a shred of history. Your history. Once you commit yourself to paper your reflections become a thing of beauty. Your beauty.

When you write online you are hiding in plain sight. When you write on paper you are exposed. A status update is a flick of the wrist, a handwritten journal is an investment. Pixels on a screen keep language locked up in a digital prison, marks on a page populate the real world.

The moment you put pen to paper you are a maker of culture not just a consumer. Writing is the one technology that makes all the others possible. And it is a physical act of creative expression, in your hands, in your power – unique to you. It confirms your species defining characteristic – you can take ideas and make them into objects. You can turn your thoughts into things – things that in time turn back into thoughts.

The empty page is the most terrifying and the most exciting thing you can possibly imagine. It's like virgin snow.

*Are you ready to bare your soul?*

# *just* *who am I?*

It's not easy navigating a course through life. Self-reflection is rapidly becoming a forgotten artform in a society obsessed with social media's mindless status updates, links, likes and superficial self-projections. While each of us is more connected to the outside world than ever before we often feel completely isolated.

***This is What My Soul Looks Like*** gives you the ability to undertake a quest to find the real you.

It's a collection of gently probing questions and prompts that lead you to uncover just exactly makes you tick.

Treat this book as a journey of discovery, a real confessional that will playfully encourage you to push your limits as you discover your unedited self.

Explore not only who you are now, but who you want to be. Consider who is here with you on your journey and ultimately just where it is that you're going.

**Think of it as DIY Therapy.**

So, if you want to find out who you really are, why not start with the question: what do you really think?

# The unexamined life is not worth living

Socrates

# *hello there*

Before we get started its important for me to tell you not what this book is but what it isn't. Make no mistake it's not meant to be some quasi-pseudo intellectual book of pop-psychology.

*OK. So what is it then?*

Well in short, It will be exactly what you make it.

## *Ultimately it's you who's the real author.*

What makes you tick? What do you think? What you feel?

Why you are who you are.

*In short. This. Book. Goes. Deeper.*

Can you talk honestly to others? Can you talk honestly to yourself?

It's your values, your beliefs and your actions that determine what happens in your life.

Be bold, be curious, be courageous and be creative, but above all, be you.

Think of this journal as a suitcase packed with your accumulated life experiences. This is your opportunity to lay out its contents and maybe put things back just a little neater and tidier than they were before.

## *Nobody knows you like you know you.*

Since you'll be answering the questions I guess logic says you should already know the answers. Well its time to find out.

Don't worry, we're all supremely biased and that's perfectly fine. Many of our decisions are subjective. Ultimately we all make choices and decisions, then we constantly try to justify them.

In short. You have to ask 'who am I' if you want any chance of finding out who you want to be. The saying goes that you can't fix something unless you know its broken.

Will the authentic you be able to find a voice free from constraints, filters and self-censorship?

*Find your voice, describe who you think you are*

# putting distance
## between
# who we think
## we are...

# ...and who we
## really are

*There are parts of us that are unfamiliar, even to ourselves.*

This is a book about introspection. It's there to scratch
beneath the surface and let our subconscious mind
get in on the action too.

While we might find it easy to understand other people we
can find it uncomfortable to try to get to know ourselves.

***Put short, we're a mass of contradictions.***

Understanding our true 'self' is difficult, its like herding cats. The picture we have of who we are at any one time is constantly being distorted, our self-image being bent out of shape by our unconscious thoughts and biases.

We are continually protecting ourselves by warping our thinking to give answers that we feel are representative of our true selves. Polarizing our thoughts into black and white or simply good and bad.

We hold back and dwell on negative self-image and continually deceive ourselves. Each one of us convinced by our truthfulness and manipulating our thinking to reinforce our own positive (or negative) views.

If we can remain true to our thoughts, beliefs and values then no matter how chaotic life is around us we have a chance. While our own flexibility is the key to overcoming and succeeding we still need a place to start from. To be able to grow, adapt and change.

So, put simply, to explore your own narrative you now find yourself playing the lead role in the story of your life. Go forward using the following pages as your character notes.

Who knows how it will unfold? It could be a drama, romance, adventure or epic. However it turns out, it will undoubtedly be peppered with an awesome, affectionate, loyal and caring supporting cast of characters.

# *7 brutal truths about self-awareness*

1. Without an ability to self-reflect, it's logical that you'll find yourself with limited self-awareness. Looking inwards helps you understand your life on the outside

2. By taking the time to ask yourself these questions you gain a deeper understanding of not only your own personal strengths and weaknesses, but also your values and beliefs. Writing can be a great healer.

3. Gain clarity and direction. Being honest allows you to solve internal conflicts, transform your thinking, gain new perspectives and deepen your understanding of who you really are.

4. Getting to the truth. To enable you to grow from your experiences you need to understand not just what's true but also what's not. Expressing our emotions is an integral part of our well-being.

5. Writing is an excellent opportunity to document your thoughts and stimulate reflection. There are no wrong answers. Put simply when thoughts are put into words learning occurs.

6. Your reflective journal should not be a once only exercise. You are constantly developing and changing. You should not only reflect on the questions but your answers too. Ask yourself often . . . are they still true?

7. If you don't self-reflect you can't challenge your resistance to change. Constantly question your personal script and ultimately your mindset. Remember, you will forever be a work in progress.

**Introvert**

*Solitude of the self*

I gain my energy from the 'internal world'

*or*

**Extrovert**

*Interaction with others*

I gain my energy from the 'external world'

# *How to use this book*

Before you start, remember that your thoughts today will be different from your thoughts yesterday and indeed your thoughts tomorrow. Every thought can be influenced by your physical, emotional and psychological context at that exact moment in time.

What we think of the past and our expectations for the future are both forces only to be found at the present time . . . in the here and now. . .

*Please don't treat this journal like a workbook. It's not. (At least its not meant to be). There are no rules.*

Your environment and mood **can** and **will** affect your answers, so to make things as relaxed as possible:

- Turn off your phone. Relax. Unplug yourself from life.

- Remember there are no wrong answers. Approach everything in a playful and curious way.

- Take time to answer each section. You can answer any question in any section and in any order at any time.

- Be patient. Don't try and work through things all at once.

- If you come across a section that you're struggling with it's fine. Skip it and come back. Be that in a day, in a week, in a month or even in a year. It's all good.

- Be honest. Be open. Be engaged. Smile. Often.
- See it as a unique opportunity to ask yourself who you really are. Trust in yourself. Be Bold.

Remember, life really is a journey that needs to be navigated with epic crests, deep troughs and choppy bits along the way.

*So, let's hoist anchor and set sail.*

*Find a quiet spot and a favourite chair.*

## Get comfy.

*Close your eyes and relax your body.*

*Make no effort to control your breathing, simply try to breathe naturally.*

*Feel the rhythm of your chest rising and falling.*

*Focus on every breath, each separate inhalation and exhalation.*

*If your mind starts to wander simply return your focus back to your breathing.*

## Count each inhale and exhale as you go.

*Do this for at least 3 minutes.*

*Slowly. Open your eyes. Stretch.*

## Pick up your pen. Pause.

*...You're ready to begin your journey.*

JUST WHO AM I?

ME

# Me

Just who am I?

Early in life we determine our own
individual conclusions as to how
to survive and the best methods
of ensuring that our needs are met.

While many of these decisions take place
in our childhood they do go on to influence and
shape us throughout the rest of our lives.

# *My life defined in 10 words*

_____

_____

_____

_____

_____

_____

_____

_____

# *I am...*

*(circle the option that you are most drawn to)*

Adventurous *or* Cautious

Conservative *or* Liberal

Ambitious *or* Laid back

Cynical *or* Idealistic

Bite my tongue *or* Speak my mind

Flexible *or* Focussed

Dreamer *or* Doer

Methodical *or* Carefree

Independent *or* Dependent

Cooperative *or* Controlling

Quality *or* Quantity

Think out loud *or* Think in my head

Competitive *or* Collaborative

Optimistic *or* Pessimistic

Disciplined *or* Spontaneous

Romantic *or* Realistic

Practical *or* Imaginative

Reactive *or* Proactive

# *Threedom*

*3 is the magic number:*

Three things that I most like about myself

1

2

3

Three things that I would like to change about myself

1

2

3

Three things that make me happy

1

2

3

Three things that give me purpose

1

2

3

Three things that I'd like to change in my life

1

2

3

*Who looks outside,*
*dreams;*
*who looks inside,*
*awakes*

Carl Jung

### *The only one...*

The one thing that I know now
that I wish that I had known then

The biggest risk I've taken

The one thing that I want most out of life

The critical turning point in my life

The question that I would rather not know the answer to

## *The only one...*

The most precious thing in my life

If I woke up tomorrow with no fear, the first thing I would do

My guilty pleasure

The lie that I tell myself the most

A bridge that I would like to burn

# *When I was a child I...*

# *One side or the other*

*(circle one option)*

Centre of attention *or* On the fringes

Children: Blessing *or* Burden

Bad news first *or* Good news first

Work to live *or* Live to work

Ask for permission *or* Request forgiveness

Lover *or* Fighter

Conventional *or* Original

Always early *or* Always late

Save *or* Spend

Go with the flow *or* Swim against the current

Form *or* Functionality

Night Owl *or* Early riser

Driven by fear of failure *or* Motivated by success

Spontaneity *or* Stability

Learn from the past *or* Focus on the future

Nature *or* Nurture

Individualism *or* Collectivism

# A (difficult) interview with you

*Life is more interesting . . . when you ask more questions.*

The one memory that I most frequently visualize

The bitterest pill I ever had to swallow

My subconscious is telling me

A time I was blind to the real truth

The challenges I face

A deep-rooted belief that I know is wrong

A feeling that is growing stronger

The burden I have carried for too long

The pain that is still raw to me

I feel powerless to

Feelings that I can't express

Things that I am resentful of

The things that I find draining


The last time I cried in public


Something I have a sneaking feeling about

# Mmmm . . . Motivation

*The things that give me the get up and go . . .*

My self worth comes from

Things that get me fired up

The one thing that I will never give up on

My heart is telling me

My head is telling me

The one thing that I'm holding on to




The things that I strive for




A fear that is driving me




A goal that is motivating me

# *Word association*

*The first word that comes to mind
when I think of the following...*

Love

Desire

Optimism

Hope

Dismay

Confusion

Fear

Rejection

Strength

Guilt

Exhaustion

Envy

Indifference

Hurt

# *Autonomy and the search for self*

[autos]  *self*

[nomos]  *law*

As individuals we strive for autonomy, our own awareness, spontaneity and the capacity for intimacy. Making new decisions and empowering ourselves to take control of our lives.

Taibi Kahler, a psychologist, identified five common drivers that motivate us as part of our personal 'script'.

Determining which of these drivers we exhibit helps us to become more aware and understand how each one influences our lives.

These drivers result in the behaviour that we exhibit in the wider world. We can each exhibit characteristics from each driver but are there any that speak loudly to you?

*Can you see yourself in any of them?*

**BE PERFECT**

**HURRY UP**

**PLEASE PEOPLE**

**BE STRONG**

**TRY HARD**

*Turn over the page to see some of their characteristics.*

# *my drivers*

**BE PERFECT** – *Drawing energy from doing the 'right things'*

I have a meticulous attention to detail

I aim to be accurate and try and get it right

I don't like losing

I'm always super organized

Appearances matter to me

I'm a good co-ordinator


**HURRY UP** – *Getting stuff done*

I 'm OK to work with tight deadlines

I'm great at multi tasking

I'm really enthusiastic/energetic

I'm OK with bending the rules

I like to dive straight in

I'm constantly spinning plates to get more done


**PLEASE OTHERS** – *The understanders*

I love meeting new people

I like to work as part of a team

I prefer to get on well with others

I'm an excellent communicator

I put other people's happiness in front of mine

I don't like to say no

**BE STRONG** – *Those with a need to cope with crisis*

I try to stay calm under pressure

I don't panic easily

I prefer to be strong

I don't like to ask for help

I'm a good negotiator

To be emotional is to be weak

I'm happy to step up and carry a heavy burden

I prefer to work alone

I'm consistent and reliable


**TRY HARD** – *Bags of enthusiasm and energy*

I'm self-motivated

I always give 100% effort

I'm resourceful and will look for alternatives

I find it uncomfortable when I'm praised

I'll try anything

I strive to improve and always get better

I like to volunteer for tasks

I get bored easily

I'm thorough in everything I do

When I start something I don't stop until I've finished it

The thing that I need to let go of




My greatest accomplishment




My most treasured possessions




The things that I'm too hard on myself about

The things in my life which are toxic

The one bad habit that I would like to break

Things that I'm currently saying yes to that I should be saying no to

I couldn't imagine living without

# *Head or Heart?*

## JUDGEMENT AND DECISION MAKING

*Are you a thinker or a feeler? Looking at the following, do you focus on just the facts or would you rather concentrate on their meaning?*

| **THINKING** | **FEELING** |
|---|---|
| Analytical | Artistic |
| Truth | Passionate |
| Rational | Warm, Personal |
| Theoretical | Ethical |
| Equal | Feelings |
| Look for flaws | Individual |
| My head rules heart | Empathic |
| Needs to be a fair and just solution | Personal Values |
| Using facts and logic | Heart over head |
| Motivated by achievement | Consider others |

*I make my judgements based upon...*

# *A letter to my childhood self*

# *My life story*

*You've been commissioned to write your autobiography. Looking at your life chronologically, what title would you give to each chapter?*

Book Title:

Chapter 1:

Chapter 2:

Chapter 3:

Chapter 4:

Chapter 5:

Chapter 6:


Chapter 7:


Chapter 8:


Chapter 9:


Chapter 10:


Epilogue:


What is the main theme of your story?
*(such as redemption, rags to riches, romance, overcoming adversity, a journey or a success story)*

# *I am someone who...*

Loves _____

Hates _____

Can't _____

Can _____

Will never _____

Will always _____

Wants _____

Needs _____

Is driven by _____

Can't wait to _____

Is happiest when _____

Wishes I could _____

Has tried to _____

Never forgets to _____

Believes in _____

Is thankful for _____

Can't get enough _____

Will one day _____

# *Milestones in my life...*

This is my calling

One thing that I take for granted

The pain I feel

The love I feel

The critical turning point in my life




The questions in my life that have remained unanswered




The things that I'm too hard on myself about




The advice I would give my 10 year old self

# *Repeat after me*

MY AFFIRMATIONS FOR LIFE

I will:

*...because I'm stronger than I thought*

I don't:

*...because it's OK to fall short and learn from my experiences*

I won't:

*...because I accept that there are some things I cannot change*

I can get through this:

*...because I have belief and confidence in myself*

---

I forgive:

*...because I want to show compassion and understanding*
*and accept others for who they are*

---

I can learn from:

*...because I will use the experience to help me learn and grow*

I will be happier when:

*...because I will focus on the positive
and endeavour to be content*

---

I forgive myself for:

*...because I strive to be the best that I can
and accept that sometimes I might fall short*

---

I accept that I cannot:

*...but I continue to focus on the positive
and make the best of each situation*

I look forward to:

*...as a commitment to having new experiences*
*and learning new things*

I am realistic that :

*...because  I accept that there are things that I cannot change*

# *Taking off the mask*

*Finish the sentence...*

I am

My dreams are

I can

I deserve

I believe in

I am ready to

I am grateful for

I accept

I believe

It's OK to

I am free to

Every day I

# *Express yourself*

My body is

My mind is

My soul is

# Counting my blessings

*The things in my life that I'm thankful for...*

# *Me, Myself, I*

## EMOTIONALLY SPEAKING

I'm angry at

I'm bored by

I'm confused by

I'm eager to

I'm envious of

I'm excited by

I'm fearful of

I'm frustrated by

I'm grateful for

I loathe

I'm proud of

I'm sad because

I'm suspicious of

I'm worried by

I hope for

I don't understand

I'm embarrassed by

I'm passionate about

## *Permission to...*

The main *do's* that I have followed in life:

# *Prohibition...*

The main *don'ts* that I have experienced in life:

# *The scale of things*

MY CHARACTERISTICS

*(make a mark on the scale where you feel you stand)*

| | | |
|---|---|---|
| Private | | Open |
| Considered | | Spontaneous |
| Curious | | Cautious |
| Organised | | Disorganised |
| Nervous | | Confident |
| Conventional | | Original |
| Contented | | Discontented |
| Ambitious | | Unambitious |
| Careless | | Careful |
| Conforming | | Independent |
| Punctual | | Relaxed |
| Loner | | Joiner |

| | | |
|---:|:---:|:---|
| Placid | └─┴─┴─┴─┴─┴─┴─┴─┴─┴─┘ | Headstrong |
| Trusting | └─┴─┴─┴─┴─┴─┴─┴─┴─┴─┘ | Jealous |
| Passive | └─┴─┴─┴─┴─┴─┴─┴─┴─┴─┘ | Active |
| Patient | └─┴─┴─┴─┴─┴─┴─┴─┴─┴─┘ | Impatient |
| Practical | └─┴─┴─┴─┴─┴─┴─┴─┴─┴─┘ | Impractical |
| Proud | └─┴─┴─┴─┴─┴─┴─┴─┴─┴─┘ | Humble |
| Bold | └─┴─┴─┴─┴─┴─┴─┴─┴─┴─┘ | Fearful |
| Compassionate | └─┴─┴─┴─┴─┴─┴─┴─┴─┴─┘ | Indifferent |
| Decisive | └─┴─┴─┴─┴─┴─┴─┴─┴─┴─┘ | Procrastinator |
| Dependable | └─┴─┴─┴─┴─┴─┴─┴─┴─┴─┘ | Inconsistent |
| Thrifty | └─┴─┴─┴─┴─┴─┴─┴─┴─┴─┘ | Extravagant |
| Tolerant | └─┴─┴─┴─┴─┴─┴─┴─┴─┴─┘ | Judgemental |

# *Self acceptance*

*Your own mind might be supremely subjective but you have to
acknowledge its mighty difficult to argue with.*

I want to feel

I want to be

I want to know

I will feel better if

I will feel respected if

My self image will be stronger if

My peace of mind will be calmed if

My relationship will be deeper if

*If you're searching for that one person who will change your life, take a look in the mirror*

anon

## *Bury it in the Vault*

You are given a sturdy box. Its incredibly heavy, made of thick panels of oak with strong hinges and an enormous steel lock.

When you have finished filling the box it will be there to hold your worries / memories / thoughts and fears and the negative baggage that you want to leave behind.

On completion the box will be sealed. It will be locked and placed in a vault buried 1000 feet underground with 6ft thick impregnable concrete walls.

*List what you would put in the box.*

# My core values

*These are the deeply held beliefs that influence our very being.
Select and circle those that speak directly to you.*

### I am who I am because of my:

| | |
|---|---|
| Accountability | Curiosity |
| Adaptability | Daring |
| Ambition | Decisiveness |
| Approachability | Dedication |
| Assertiveness | Dependability |
| Awareness | Determination |
| Balance | Devotion |
| Calmness | Diligence |
| Caution | Dignity |
| Commitment | Discipline |
| Compassion | Discretion |
| Confidence | Efficiency |
| Conviction | Empathy |
| Contentedness | Experience |
| Cooperation | Enthusiasm |
| Courage | Faithfulness |
| Creativity | Fidelity |

| | |
|---|---|
| Focus | Privacy |
| Fun | Punctuality |
| Generosity | Rationality |
| Happiness | Realism |
| Hardwork | Religion |
| Honesty | Reason |
| Hope | Resilience |
| Humility | Resourcefulness |
| Imagination | Respect |
| Independence | Responsibility |
| Integrity | Self discipline |
| Kindness | Self-reliance |
| Leadership | Sensitivity |
| Loyalty | Spirituality |
| Mindfulness | Spontaneity |
| Modesty | Stability |
| Motivation | Strength |
| Openness | Success |
| Optimism | Thoughtfulness |
| Organisation | Tolerance |
| Originality | Understanding |
| Passion | Trust |
| Patience | Wisdom |
| Perception | |
| Persistence | |

## *Ain't that the truth...*

*Well, at least what do you believe?*

When I think of the past I

When I think of you I

When I need inspiration I

When I think about unconditional love I think of

When I think of suffering I

When I'm frightened I

When I need courage I

When I think of the future I

The best piece of advice that I have been given

The advice I would give

YOU ARE ALL HERE WITH ME

# You

Who's here with me?

Family, friends and relationships shape and mould us into who we are.

But social media can trick us into thinking that their multitude of connections are more valuable than the small number of bonds that we hold with those that really matter in our life.

We lose out on the feeling of really bonding with those close to us, really missing them, missing their physical presence and the things that make them who they are and what they mean to us.

That feeling of longing that used to make us write letters to each other on paper is lost.

# *My journey*

Our personal relationships are anchored in trust, empathy, compassion, humility and empathy.

You have two pages. Fill each one with the connections in your life. The people that have nurtured you, love you and have in their own way shaped you all through your life.

# *Looking behind the mask*

*We can be different things to different people for different reasons at different times.*

How I am like my mother/guardian

How I am like my father/guardian

The questions I wish I could ask my parents/guardians

The person who shaped the course of my life the most


My guardian angel


The people who have pulled me through


The person that inspires me to do better

The things (and people) that I've wasted my time on

The person I'm most proud of

The person whose judgement I trust

The person I respect

The relationships that I need to resurrect

The person that I have given up on


The person that knows me better than anyone else


The greatest love of my life


The person I would trust with my life


The most memorable lesson that I learned from my parents


The personality trait that I value the most in others

The person that makes me feel invisible


The people who inspire me


The person whom I should give one more chance


The person who always had faith in me

# *The future is calling*

*In 10 year's time I will...*

Be focussed on _____

Be celebrating _____

Be living in _____

Be working as _____

Be interested in _____

Be needing _____

Be learning _____

Be a successful _____

Be serious about _____

Be having fun with _____

Be on the path to _____

Be still in touch with _____

Be trying to find _____

Be happy to have left _____

Be mastering _____

Be trying to change _____

Be laughing at _____

Be thankful for _____

Be missing _____

# *Only you...*

FOR .............................................................................

In the past you were . . .

When will you  . . .

When you're not there I . . .

When will you appreciate my . . .

When you lie . . .


In the future we will  . . .


Your expectations are . . .


I love your . . .


Our foundations are . . .

# *Yearning, craving, longing, wishing*

## AN INVENTORY OF WANTS OVER NEEDS

I want to feel valued by

I want to feel respected by

I want to feel loved by

I want to build a connection with

I want to stop the pain from

I want to feel accepted by

I want to heal my relationship with

# *The givers in my life*

Those that give more than they take.

## *The takers in my life*

Those that take more than they give.

# *These are my people*

THE PERSON/PEOPLE THAT...

Make me laugh

Love me

Value my opinion

I confide in

I have fun with

Influence me

Lead me astray

Suck the life out of me

Guide me

Make me feel like a child again

Know me better than anyone else

The one person in my life that I wish I'd met sooner

My friends from my teenage years

Those that give me their unconditional love

# It's OK to be OK

## and

## It's OK to be NOT OK

GIVING A VOICE TO MY THOUGHTS, FEELINGS
AND EMOTIONS

*It's OK to laugh and cry, feel loved and lonely, feel guilty and
ecstatic, feel sensitive and indifferent.*

I feel loved when

I'm suspicious of

I'm numb to

I feel smart when

I'm worried by

I feel healthy when

I'm terrified by

I feel safe when

I'm indifferent to

I feel creative when

I'm desperate to

I trust

I feel betrayed by

I feel comforted by

I'm skeptical of

I'm in awe of

I'm embarrassed by

I'm interested in

I'm confused by

I'm pessimistic about

I feel special when

I feel guilty for

I feel daring when

I care about

I don't care about

I'm surprised by

I'm envious of

I'm curious to

I regret

I feel decadent when

I'm shocked by

I respect

I'm bored by

I feel powerful when

I feel let down by

I feel spiritual when

I detest

I'm desperate to

I'm fed up with

I feel free when

I feel useless when

I feel a sense of accomplishment when

*What is a friend?*

*A single soul dwelling in two bodies*

Aristotle

# Treasures expressed

*The 10 closest people in my life
described in one word*

Name                                          Described

_____          .............................

_____          .............................

_____          .............................

_____          .............................

_____          .............................

_____          .............................

_____          .............................

_____          .............................

_____          .............................

_____          .............................

A time in my life that I should have tried harder

The person that I trust implicitly

If I could ask one person one question and they had to answer 100% truthfully, this is who I would ask and this is what I would ask

Someone who my needs my help

The teacher that inspired me

The people that I have loved and lost

The people I am most connected to

If I could go back and fix one relationship it would be

The relationships that require more of my time and effort

A relationship that I would like to improve

...and the first step to improving that relationship

# *Me, Myself, I*

*Match a thought (or a person) to the feeling*

I feel affection for . . . . . . . . . . . . . . . . . . . . . . . . . . . . . . . . . . . . . .

I'm attracted by/to . . . . . . . . . . . . . . . . . . . . . . . . . . . . . . . . . . . .

I'm compassionate towards . . . . . . . . . . . . . . . . . . . . . . . . . . .

I desire . . . . . . . . . . . . . . . . . . . . . . . . . . . . . . . . . . . . . . . . . . . . . . . .

I feel sympathy for . . . . . . . . . . . . . . . . . . . . . . . . . . . . . . . . . . . .

I'm passionate about . . . . . . . . . . . . . . . . . . . . . . . . . . . . . . . . . .

I love . . . . . . . . . . . . . . . . . . . . . . . . . . . . . . . . . . . . . . . . . . . . . . . . .

I care for . . . . . . . . . . . . . . . . . . . . . . . . . . . . . . . . . . . . . . . . . . . . .

I nurture . . . . . . . . . . . . . . . . . . . . . . . . . . . . . . . . . . . . . . . . . . . . .

I pity . . . . . . . . . . . . . . . . . . . . . . . . . . . . . . . . . . . . . . . . . . . . . . . . .

I'm infatuated by . . . . . . . . . . . . . . . . . . . . . . . . . . . . . . . . . . . . .

I'm nostalgic for . . . . . . . . . . . . . . . . . . . . . . . . . . . . . . . . . . . . . .

I'm protective of . . . . . . . . . . . . . . . . . . . . . . . . . . . . . . . . . . . . . .

I'm indulgent with . . . . . . . . . . . . . . . . . . . . . . . . . . . . . . . . . . . .

I'm ecstatic about . . . . . . . . . . . . . . . . . . . . . . . . . . . . . . . . . . . . .

I have a zest for . . . . . . . . . . . . . . . . . . . . . . . . . . . . . . . . . . . . . . .

# *Everything I know I learned from...*

*Friends/family/lovers/haters/makers/doers/teachers
and others. The people who have made me who I am today.*

............................................................makes me laugh

............................................................stresses me out

............................................................makes me feel alive

............................................................makes me feel wanted

............................................................brings me joy

............................................................makes me cry

............................................................makes me happy

............................................................makes me feel useful

............................................................makes me despair

............................................................gives me hope

............................................................makes me optimistic

............................................................gives me a sense of belonging

............................................................disappoints me

............................................................makes me miserable

............................................................broke my heart

# *Expressions*

*Dig deep and consider...*

A casual relationship that needs nurturing:

. . . . . . . . . . . . . . . . . . . . . . . . . . . . . . . . . . . . . . . . . . . . . . . . . . . . . .

The deepest connection I have to someone:

. . . . . . . . . . . . . . . . . . . . . . . . . . . . . . . . . . . . . . . . . . . . . . . . . . . . . .

A deep-seated dislike of someone, which I know is wrong:

. . . . . . . . . . . . . . . . . . . . . . . . . . . . . . . . . . . . . . . . . . . . . . . . . . . . . .

The one person that I will always protect fiercely

. . . . . . . . . . . . . . . . . . . . . . . . . . . . . . . . . . . . . . . . . . . . . . . . . . . . . .

Someone I have heartfelt love for

. . . . . . . . . . . . . . . . . . . . . . . . . . . . . . . . . . . . . . . . . . . . . . . . . . . . . .

I feel sentimental when I think about

. . . . . . . . . . . . . . . . . . . . . . . . . . . . . . . . . . . . . . . . . . . . . . . . . . . . . .

A time when I felt raw emotion overwhelm me

. . . . . . . . . . . . . . . . . . . . . . . . . . . . . . . . . . . . . . . . . . . . . .

A damaging relationship that I'm reluctant to end

. . . . . . . . . . . . . . . . . . . . . . . . . . . . . . . . . . . . . . . . . . . . . .

I feel real remorse when I think of

. . . . . . . . . . . . . . . . . . . . . . . . . . . . . . . . . . . . . . . . . . . . . .

I feel betrayed by

. . . . . . . . . . . . . . . . . . . . . . . . . . . . . . . . . . . . . . . . . . . . . .

My belief is unshaken in

. . . . . . . . . . . . . . . . . . . . . . . . . . . . . . . . . . . . . . . . . . . . . .

With all my heart and soul I

. . . . . . . . . . . . . . . . . . . . . . . . . . . . . . . . . . . . . . . . . . . . . .

My greatest strength

. . . . . . . . . . . . . . . . . . . . . . . . . . . . . . . . . . . . . . . . . . . . . .

TOO SHORT TO WORRY
TOO LONG TO WAIT

LIFE

# Life

The here and now

When we rise above the realm of necessity and survival to catch those ineffable moments of peak experience, we feel from time to time that there is much more meaning to life.

But there is the question, how do we integrate that into our everyday lives?

How do we stoke the embers to bring the fire to life?

How do we create a bridge between who we are and who we really want to be?

Where do we find the buried treasure?

# *The future starts now*

*What are you waiting for...*
*The things that I need to start...today*

The person to call

The change to make

The conversation to have

The question to ask

The journey to plan

The goal to set

The commitment to make

The baggage to let go of

The thing to forget

The promise to make

The person to thank

The plans to make

The risk to take

# Don't stop believing

*Trust, faith and confidence will take you as far as you need to go,*
*even if the destination seems out of reach right now.*

I believe in

I believe I can

I believe in being

I believe I have the power to

I believe I have the right to be

I believe everyone is

I believe in having

# *It's OK...*

*However you feel, its OK to...*

It's OK to . . . . . . . . . . . . . . . . . . . . . . . . . . . . . . . . . . . . . . . . . . . . . .

It's OK that I . . . . . . . . . . . . . . . . . . . . . . . . . . . . . . . . . . . . . . . . . . . .

It's OK when . . . . . . . . . . . . . . . . . . . . . . . . . . . . . . . . . . . . . . . . . . . . .

It's OK for me to say . . . . . . . . . . . . . . . . . . . . . . . . . . . . . . . . . . . . . . .

It's OK for me to ask for . . . . . . . . . . . . . . . . . . . . . . . . . . . . . . . . . . . .

It's Ok to say no to . . . . . . . . . . . . . . . . . . . . . . . . . . . . . . . . . . . . . . . . .

It's OK to let go of . . . . . . . . . . . . . . . . . . . . . . . . . . . . . . . . . . . . . . . . . .

It's OK to start again with . . . . . . . . . . . . . . . . . . . . . . . . . . . . . . . . . . .

It's OK to move on from . . . . . . . . . . . . . . . . . . . . . . . . . . . . . . . . . . . . .

### *It's OK to be not OK*

# *There can only be one*

One thing that I'm most proud of

. . . . . . . . . . . . . . . . . . . . . . . . . . . . . . . . . . . . . . . . . . . . . . . . .

One thing in life that I just can't live without

. . . . . . . . . . . . . . . . . . . . . . . . . . . . . . . . . . . . . . . . . . . . . . . . .

One thing in life that I will never do

. . . . . . . . . . . . . . . . . . . . . . . . . . . . . . . . . . . . . . . . . . . . . . . . .

One thing in life that I love doing but I never do anymore

. . . . . . . . . . . . . . . . . . . . . . . . . . . . . . . . . . . . . . . . . . . . . . . . .

One responsibility that I wish I didn't have to deal with

. . . . . . . . . . . . . . . . . . . . . . . . . . . . . . . . . . . . . . . . . . . . . . . . .

One thing that I take for granted every day

. . . . . . . . . . . . . . . . . . . . . . . . . . . . . . . . . . . . . . . . . . . . . . . . .

One thing that humanity should be trying to solve

. . . . . . . . . . . . . . . . . . . . . . . . . . . . . . . . . . . . . . . . . . . . . . . . .

One thing that is holding me back from being
the person I want to be

. . . . . . . . . . . . . . . . . . . . . . . . . . . . . . . . . . . . . . . . . . . . . . . . .

One thing that they should teach you in school but don't

. . . . . . . . . . . . . . . . . . . . . . . . . . . . . . . . . . . . . . . . . . . . . . . . .

# *There can only be one*

One thing that I always procrastinate over

. . . . . . . . . . . . . . . . . . . . . . . . . . . . . . . . . . . . . . . . . . . . .

One thing that I'm most determined to do in my life

. . . . . . . . . . . . . . . . . . . . . . . . . . . . . . . . . . . . . . . . . . . . .

One controversial opinion I have

. . . . . . . . . . . . . . . . . . . . . . . . . . . . . . . . . . . . . . . . . . . . .

One thing that I'm superstitious about

. . . . . . . . . . . . . . . . . . . . . . . . . . . . . . . . . . . . . . . . . . . . .

One time in my life when I just knew it was fate

. . . . . . . . . . . . . . . . . . . . . . . . . . . . . . . . . . . . . . . . . . . . .

One thing that overwhelms me

. . . . . . . . . . . . . . . . . . . . . . . . . . . . . . . . . . . . . . . . . . . . .

One thing that I take for granted

. . . . . . . . . . . . . . . . . . . . . . . . . . . . . . . . . . . . . . . . . . . . .

One thing that I just can't relate to

. . . . . . . . . . . . . . . . . . . . . . . . . . . . . . . . . . . . . . . . . . . . .

One thing I believe in

. . . . . . . . . . . . . . . . . . . . . . . . . . . . . . . . . . . . . . . . . . . . .

The age I feel


Success should be measured by



If all jobs paid the same wage, I would choose to be a



If I had to dedicate myself to a cause it would be



The last time I saw something I didn't agree with and chose
not to speak up

The place I go for serenity

My greatest source of inspiration

My greatest achievement

# *Changes ahead*

*Remember nothing will change if nothing changes*

Things that I want to change and I can change easily

Things that I want to change but that will require a lot of effort

Things that I want to change but am unable to

Things that I no longer want to be responsible for

The setback that I will overcome

The aspect of my personality that I need to work on

# *Words of wisdom*

*Think fast. Better still don't think at all. Sidestep your own mental filters and say it like it is. Write down the first word that comes to mind when you think of...*

Wealth

Obligation

Opportunity

Success

Purpose

Dreams

Freedom

Power

Lies

Pleasure

Fear

Joy _____

Destiny _____

Health _____

Change _____

Harmony _____

Impossible _____

Failure _____

Acceptance _____

Discipline _____

Inspiration _____

Pain _____

Compromise _____

Corruption _____

Love _____

Community _____

## *Pulling back the veil*

Things that I'm responsible for

The question that has remained unanswered

The dream that I had that has died

The one thing that I'm not prepared to give up on

The one sentence that if said would alleviate my suffering

The things in life that bring me pure and unadulterated joy

The things that break my heart

The stuff that I just can't be bothered with

I could make improvements to my life by

The time when my innocence was lost

The thing that I have lived to regret

The past events that feed my insecurities

The love I feel

The harsh truths that I have chosen to ignore

Injustices that I see in the world

The events in the past that are hindering my life in the present

One thing that I have always thought was pointless

My small pleasures in life

# More than words

*The words that speak to me right here, right now.*
*Finish these sentences...*

I'm hopeful

I'm grateful

I'm burned out

I'm comfortable

I'm satisfied

I've forgotten

I'm tired

I've ignored

I've rejected

I'm optimistic

I'm pessimistic

I'm blessed

I'm exhausted

I'm determined

I'm bored

I'm focused

I'm inspired

I'm depressed

I'm renewed

I'm dejected

# my morality meter

## *versus*

# my ethical dilemmas

Hey, who doesn't live by their own moral code?

# *This is how I feel about...*

|  | acceptable | wrong |
|---|---|---|
| Birth Control | . . . . . | . . . . . |
| Divorce | . . . . . | . . . . . |
| Gambling | . . . . . | . . . . . |
| Embryonic Stem Cell Research | . . . . . | . . . . . |
| Recreational Drugs | . . . . . | . . . . . |
| The Death Penalty | . . . . . | . . . . . |
| Animal Fur Clothing | . . . . . | . . . . . |
| Doctor Assisted Suicide | . . . . . | . . . . . |
| Medical Testing on Animals | . . . . . | . . . . . |
| Abortion | . . . . . | . . . . . |
| Pornography | . . . . . | . . . . . |
| Animal Cloning | . . . . . | . . . . . |
| Genetically Modified Food | . . . . . | . . . . . |
| Polygamy | . . . . . | . . . . . |
| Suicide | . . . . . | . . . . . |
| Censorship | . . . . . | . . . . . |
| The Death Penalty | . . . . . | . . . . . |

*While morals are based upon communal views of
what is right and wrong, your ethics are your own view of what
is right or wrong.*

# *Morality*

*Morals are simply codes of conduct established in society as accepted models for behaviour. Our free will is the capacity for us to make our own choices regarding our actions.*

|  | agree | disagree |
|---|---|---|
| Taking a human life can be justified | . . . . . | . . . . . |
| Animals have rights | . . . . . | . . . . . |
| There is a difference between justice and revenge | . . . . . | . . . . . |
| The rich have a moral right to help the poor | . . . . . | . . . . . |
| Same sex couples should be allowed to marry | . . . . . | . . . . . |
| Crime penalties should be more severe | . . . . . | . . . . . |
| AI is a threat to humanity | . . . . . | . . . . . |
| Immigration should be limited | . . . . . | . . . . . |

|  | agree | disagree |
|---|---|---|
| Lying to hurt someones' feeling is acceptable | · · · · · | · · · · · |
| Population control is needed | · · · · · | · · · · · |
| If a family member committed a crime I would turn them in | · · · · · | · · · · · |
| Meat is Murder | · · · · · | · · · · · |
| Karma is real | · · · · · | · · · · · |
| The internet should be censored | · · · · · | · · · · · |
| There is no such thing as climate change | · · · · · | · · · · · |
| Drugs should be legalized | · · · · · | · · · · · |
| Anyone should have the right to bear arms | · · · · · | · · · · · |

# *My goals*

SET GOAL ... PLAN GOAL ... GO!

My health goal _____

My financial goal _____

My family goal _____

My personal goal _____

My learning goal _____

My self development goal _____

My relationship goal _____

My environmental goal _____

My friendship goal _____

My career goal _____

My creative goal _____

# *Ethical dilemmas*

*Open up and tell it like it is. Choose the first word
that comes to mind when you think of.*

Euthanasia

Addiction

Discrimination

Religion

Artificial intelligence

Zoos

Organ donation

Taxes

Politics

Recreational drugs

War

Healthcare

Human rights

Climate change

Social media

Whistleblowers

Migration

Cosmetic surgery

# *Love is the answer*

*Be it passion for, a yearning to, an infatuation with*
*or devotion to . . . Love can conquer all*

I would love to learn more about

I would love to go to

I would love to try

I would love to make

I would love to see



I would love to learn to



I would love to change



I would love to stop



I would love to be

# *More than words II*

The words that speak to me right here, right now.
Finish these sentences...

I'm loved . . . . . . . . . . . . . . . . . . . . . . . . . . . . . . . . . . . . . . . . . . . . . . . . . . . . . .

I'm frustrated . . . . . . . . . . . . . . . . . . . . . . . . . . . . . . . . . . . . . . . . . . . . . . . . . .

I'm empowered . . . . . . . . . . . . . . . . . . . . . . . . . . . . . . . . . . . . . . . . . . . . . . . . .

I'm insecure . . . . . . . . . . . . . . . . . . . . . . . . . . . . . . . . . . . . . . . . . . . . . . . . . . .

I'm guarded . . . . . . . . . . . . . . . . . . . . . . . . . . . . . . . . . . . . . . . . . . . . . . . . . . . .

I'm guilty . . . . . . . . . . . . . . . . . . . . . . . . . . . . . . . . . . . . . . . . . . . . . . . . . . . . . .

I'm excited . . . . . . . . . . . . . . . . . . . . . . . . . . . . . . . . . . . . . . . . . . . . . . . . . . . . .

I'm impatient . . . . . . . . . . . . . . . . . . . . . . . . . . . . . . . . . . . . . . . . . . . . . . . . . . .

I'm alone . . . . . . . . . . . . . . . . . . . . . . . . . . . . . . . . . . . . . . . . . . . . . . . . . . . . . .

I'm calm . . . . . . . . . . . . . . . . . . . . . . . . . . . . . . . . . . . . . . . . . . . . . . . . . . . . . . .

I'm burdened . . . . . . . . . . . . . . . . . . . . . . . . . . . . . . . . . . . . . . . . . . . . . .

I'm cautious . . . . . . . . . . . . . . . . . . . . . . . . . . . . . . . . . . . . . . . . . . . . . .

I'm galvanised . . . . . . . . . . . . . . . . . . . . . . . . . . . . . . . . . . . . . . . . . . . .

I'm sorrowful . . . . . . . . . . . . . . . . . . . . . . . . . . . . . . . . . . . . . . . . . . . . .

I'm confident . . . . . . . . . . . . . . . . . . . . . . . . . . . . . . . . . . . . . . . . . . . . .

I'm positive . . . . . . . . . . . . . . . . . . . . . . . . . . . . . . . . . . . . . . . . . . . . . . .

I'm lost . . . . . . . . . . . . . . . . . . . . . . . . . . . . . . . . . . . . . . . . . . . . . . . . . . .

I'm liberated . . . . . . . . . . . . . . . . . . . . . . . . . . . . . . . . . . . . . . . . . . . . . .

I'm angry . . . . . . . . . . . . . . . . . . . . . . . . . . . . . . . . . . . . . . . . . . . . . . . . .

I'm fired up . . . . . . . . . . . . . . . . . . . . . . . . . . . . . . . . . . . . . . . . . . . . . . .

## *Everything starts with a single step*

The small steps that I could take today...

...and the first step to making that improvement

Large steps that I plan to take tomorrow...

...and the first step to making that improvement

The things I would do if I knew I couldn't fail...

...and the first step to making that improvement

My epic plan for the future...

...and the first step towards that improvement

# A list of things
## that I want to achieve in life

# My life line

Global life expectancy in 2019 was estimated to be **72.6 years** by The United Nations.

Each circle represents a month in your life
between birth and 73 years of age.

*Colour in your journey.*

# this is what
# my soul
# looks like

Life is short . . .

. . . but every morning I have a new chance.